Confessions of Smalltown

A Collection of Poems

Volume 1

By Donna Mitchell

Copyright @ 2024 Donna Mitchell

All rights reserved. No part of this publication may be reproduced, stored in a retrieval system, or transmitted, in any form or by any means, electronic, mechanical, photocopying, recording or otherwise, without the prior permission of the copyright owner.

This book is a work of fiction. Names, characters, places, and incidents either are products of the author's imagination or are used fictitiously, and any resemblance to actual events or persons, living or dead, is entirely coincidental

Confessions of Smalltown
A Collection of Poems
Volume 1

Confessions of Smalltown is set on the model characters that live in our garden railway. This is a collection of poems on all their shenanigans.

This started in 2020 during the COVID-19 Lockdown as a bit of light hearted entertainment for friends and family on social media. However, as our following grew, we decided to keep this up and turn it into a book.

Volume 1 is a collection of poems from 2020 to 2021, future volumes will include up to date poems.

Please note that Confessions of Smalltown does include some crude situations and language, therefore this is not recommended for younger readers.

For more poems, pictures, videos and regular updates on Smalltown, follow us on Facebook!

Dedicated to my dad

Donald Dowding

February 26th 1935 – April 30th 2022

Such a beautiful sight to see
Smalltown Chapel, growing fast
Weddings, meetings
Lilly mays confessions

A meeting place for all
Such a wonderful added addition
Crafts shows, tea dance
Even a summer ball

Now Lilly May she likes the Vicar
A very good-looking chap
She doesn't have any chance
Sitting on his lap

The only interest he has
Is Smalltown community
And not Lilly Mays
Constant nudity

Think she'll visit every day
To confess all her sins
She'll have no chance
The vicar won't let her in

Well unless he takes a liking to her
When she tells her stories
Thats our Lilly May
A right Jackanory.

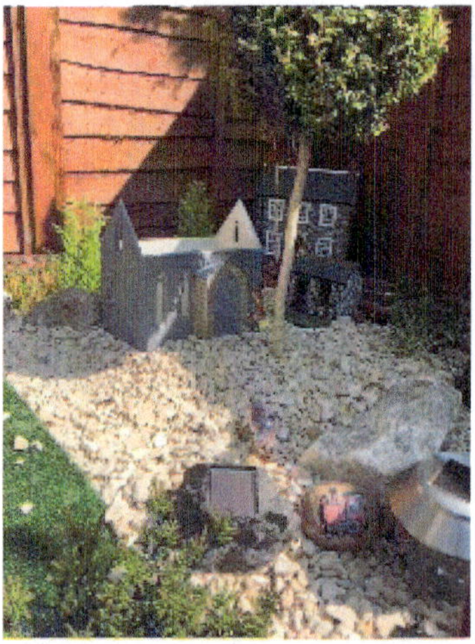

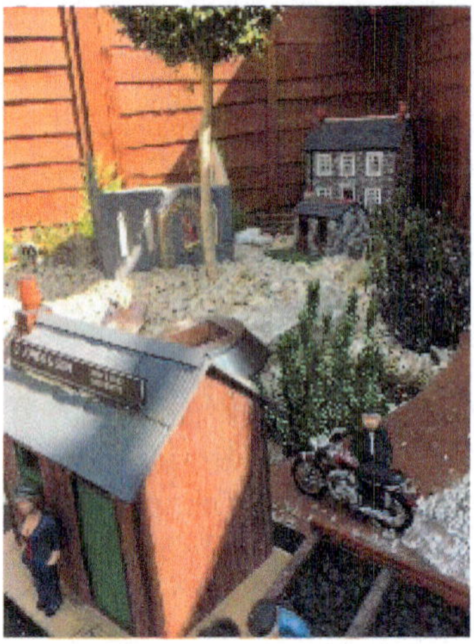

The rains come down
Lilly mays outdoors
She's definitely
Not wearing drawers

She's in the station with Randy Ron,
Pretty much all her clothes have gone
All that's left is her overshirt
Randy Ron's took off her skirt

She's very hot
That's what she'll say
But we all know, Lilly May

Randy Ron, he has a good life
16 Kids, and a great wife
Now if he's not careful; and messing about
We know his wife will kick him out

So, let's just hope, he's telling Lilly May
She needs to go back home today
She came between Ethel and Stan; now poor old
Ethel has no man.

So, watch this space
Ethels coming for her man
That will mean; shits going to hit the fan.

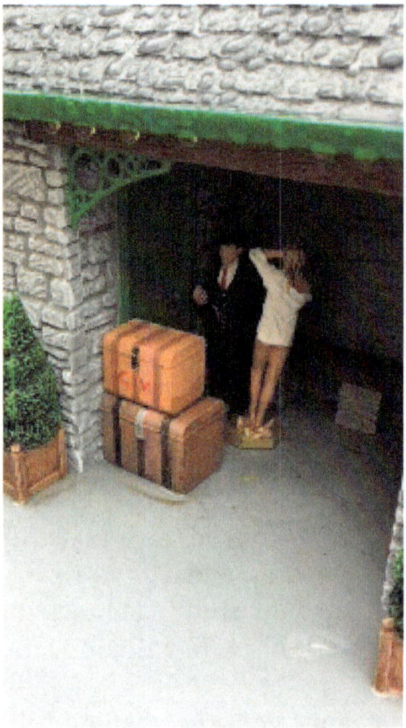

Smalltown copper he was not happy
He had lots to say
Now you know there is a lockdown
So many men coming and going at Lilly mays

Now Lilly you are not good
You're playing quite the fool
You know because of covid
No one can break the rules

Now I know it affects your business
I know you think it's not right
I know you're losing money
With the ladies of the night

But Lilly, I'm telling you
Stop being a bit of a knob
Just look at the signal box
You need to be good just like Bob.

See why old Ethel
Don't want Stan back
Look at the car
It belongs to Jack

He is a landlord of a great pub
And met ole Ethel in a London strip club
He remembers the day he put money in her bra
Then gave her a lift home in his sports car

He went to her flat picked up her luggage
Knowing Ethel came with baggage
He knew that she was with child
And had a passed of being wild

He knew he could be a good man
And a great replacement for old Stan
Now Jack plans to buy a big place, so Ethel lives
no life of disgrace

Bet ole Stan
Wish he had her life
But she's now jacks
Trouble and Strife.

As little Nelly's Nan
Stands by the wishing well
In her head
She has a Story to tell

What would she wish for
What's really on her mind
A way out of the virus
To all Mankind

Start to go out again
Meet family and friends
She really wishes
The virus to come to an end

But all she can think about
Life for her could be hell
Because 2 years ago
She pushed her husband down the Well.

We knew owe Jack had money
Now he's bringing his horses that he bred
They must be worth a fortune
Beautiful Thoroughbred

Now he likes a little bet
But breeding racehorses is his plan
Owe Ethel she's done bloody well
leaving Stan for this man

He's going to bring his Riches to this little town
He was also talking about a strip club
Or maybe buy the local pub

Now I don't know
If the town folk will be happy with all of this
Drunken old town folk
Half-naked men and women on the piss

Now Lilly May she'll be very happy
She's liking a dance or two
Swinging around a pole
Is what she loves to do

Maybe the men of the village
Will be happy with Jacks plans
But there's some really funny council people in
Smalltown

So, Jack don't get your hopes up
A strip club in the town
No way will they let men and woman
Pull their undies up and down.

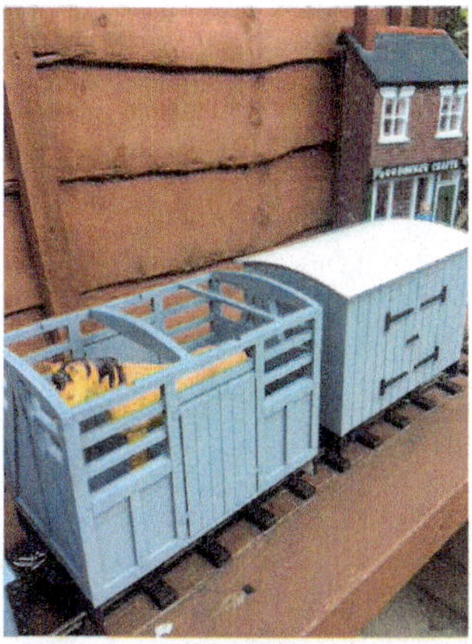

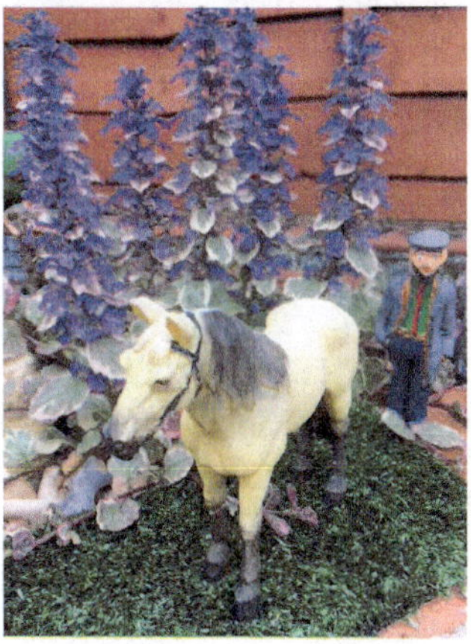

Well, the time is nearly here
And the bike shop nearly done
Great new shop
Charlie's and Sons

The inside of the shop
Theres so much more to do
Putting up the banners
Add a Flag or Two

Every bike will be advertised
And our Facebook page
Or come straight to the shop
And ride it straight away

Grifter BMXs, racing bikes as well
Tandems and electric bikes
Some choppers as well
So come visit Charlie

He's a fantastic chap
He knows everything about pushbikes
Won't fill you full of crap

He'll measure your inside leg
Check the bike will fit
Make sure it's not too big
So, you don't go ass over tit.

Charlie's and Sons
Bikes moving in
Great bike in the window
A beautiful Schwinn

We have stock in the shop
Or you can order on line
I can get them to you
In plenty of time

We do all repairs
Services too
Whatever your needs
It's up to you

When lockdown is over
We will be ready to go
Selling bikes
Putting some on show

I'm arranging a bike display
Bikes galore
New saddles for comfort
Which will stop saddle sore

Now once a year
A lot of us meet
We spent a weekend
A great drunken treat

We display all our bikes
In the show and shine
We have cups for the winners
Last year it was mine

We finish the day
Have a party for all
So come join our yearly bike show
It's one hell of a Ball.

The wind blew crazy late last night
Gave the village quite a fright
Lilly May landed in Berts lap
What a shock, such a quiet chap

Her shirt it went up round her head
She nearly left ole Bert for dead
The copper landed down the Well
He thought he was going to Hell

Oh, Boris he said, be Alert
But Lilly led on top of Bert
The coppers, head first down the Well
The Village nearly said farewell

No social distancing here again
And Smalltown witnessed a hurricane
So today a clean-up had to be
Fallen over Characters and brought down trees

But everyone survived quite well
And brought the copper back up from the well

Stay Alert, don't be like Bert.

Now Charlie has to deal with Lilly
Although he knows she's being silly
I wonder what she would like
Don't think it will be a bike

Now she's being watched by the copper
But Lilly mays, after Charlie's Chopper

It's not just the bike she wants to ride
As Charlie takes oh Lilly inside
He shut the door
And closed the blinds
We know what's on Charlie's mind

He'll give her a service
The best she's had
That will make oh Lilly glad
Oh, Lilly checking Charlie's R nuts
He's gone into quite a Rut

She's still not interested in a bike
Just a cuddle with Charlie's is what she likes
Now Charlie's sissy bars got stuck
Charlie, he has all the Luck

Wow look at Lilly's smile
She's not cycled for a while
She left the shop
Without a ride
But we all know what went on inside.

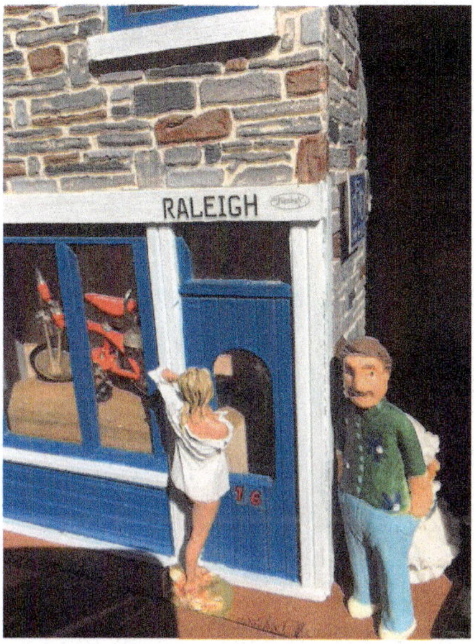
RALEIGH

A wedding was planned today
Because of the virus
It's been delayed
No one told poor old Gary
He turned up with best man Barry

There was no bride to be seen
Just Jolly Jean the Vicar drag Queen
He tried to calm Gary down
Explained it's because of lockdown

He's dressed up
Speech all done
But here he stands without no one
So had Gary been took for a ride
Stitched up by his future bride

He treated her like she was the best
Perhaps it was that old string vest
I had no bad habits that for sure
Perhaps maybe because I snore

Outside the church Gary's phone did go
It was his bank
Gary said OH NO
Gary said I'M IN THE SHIT
She's took me money all of it

Hold on while I take a look, the vicar said
No wedding was ever booked
The drag Queen vicar said now your free
Perhaps you would like to marry me

Gary said you're having a laugh
I'm not going to be your other half
Here's your dress that's not mine
And shove your lipstick where the sun doesn't shine.

What you doing up that ladder
Lilly May might be in the shower
She's just had a new Bathroom put in
We remember all the din

Now we know Stans not a window cleaner
He's hoping he can see her
Get down that ladder Randy Stan
You dirty filthy nosey man

Lilly May she knows your there
To be honest she won't care
Go careful as you come down
Oh shit, oh dear, you've hit the ground

OMG, I thought you were dead
Massive bump right on your head
Now you better get off home
You're a very naughty Peeping Tom.

Now Bert the ticket collector
In charge of the new station
Lilly popped into see him
He ended up in total frustration

Now as much as Bert really likes her
He knows she's been around
If he gives her a ticket
His feet won't touch the ground

Now this is a brand-new station
And we don't want bad stories heard
Bert canoodling with Lilly May
Would really be absurd

Now Bert was so surprised
When Lilly May said give me your ticket
His eyes popped out his head
As she grabbed his middle wicket

Omg Lilly how far do you need to go
I'll print your ticket out
I hope this trains on a go slow

The train pulled in the station
The driver came out of the train
Bert came walking out
Seriously in pain

When the train pulled up
Bert got a bad surprise
He pulled up his trousers
Caught his manhood in his flies

He shouted very loudly
Give out one hell of a scream
Just at that moment
The train let out its steam

So, all there is to say to you
You shocked me really Bert
You tarnished the new station
I'm glad your manhood hurts.

Omg there's a shock at Lilly mays
The number of ladies a surprise
This will really upset
All of Smalltown wives

Now Lusha Lee has stayed there
But that's another story to be told
Another lady of the night
Little Cassey Gold

Now there's been a council meeting so many at the hall
all the wives said it's a bloody free for all

We don't need this in the village
There are loose women all up there
Poor ole Mabel got upset
Fainted in the chair

Now, now Moody Mabel
Don't let this get you down
Well, I'm telling you
Touch my Reg, and their feet won't touch the ground

Now the wives they got together
Shirley with her hairy chin
Said this is disgusting
What's going on is a SIN

Now Vera she was fuming
Although her husband said his wife looks like a bloke

She clipped him around the head
Poor bugger nearly choked

Now we know someone has visited there
You'll be surprised it's Jolly Jean
She wants a bit of fun
And to be part of the scene

Lilly said, there's money to be made
And loads if you can
Don't know about ole Jean
As we all know she's a man

Now I got me camera out
Done a photo shoot
But I think ole Lilly May
Will give Jolly Jean the boot

Or maybe men might like Jean
Now may find her lots of fun
Because if you think about it
They get two for the price of one.

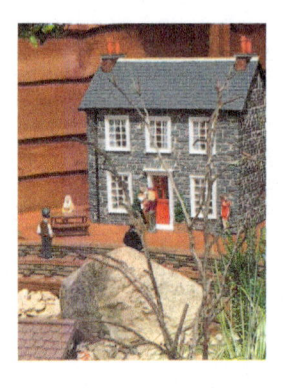

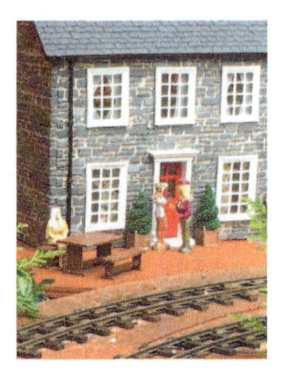

There's a lot of visitors in Smalltown
Smart couple, photographer as well
Don't know what they are doing
Only time will tell

They had lots of paperwork
Looks like some plans
Talking about workmen
And storing caravans

Now there is talk of a Newtown
A few feet down the track
All I heard them say
Their waiting for feedback

This is so exciting
Another village on the go
We will have to wait to see the plans
I'm sure they'll go on show

Just when they were talking
Along came Lilly May
I overheard her say to them
Of course
My house they can stay

So here we go again
The builders will be fine for the night
Of course, they all will
In a house with the ladies of the night.

Yesterday the train pulled up
And gets off Emmanuel
Looking absolutely gorgeous
But she's just been let out of jail

Now Lilly May she met her
Off to the house she went
She was only there 5 minutes
then she went off with a gent

Now no one knows about her
Or what her job will be
But the men of Smalltown
Definitely like what they see

Now she's a beautiful lady
And she's hard as nails
The wives of Smalltown are fishing for details

Now we all know of Lilly May
And her life that she leads
Emmanuel aims high
In life she will succeed

So, we need lots more info
Of what goes on behind closed doors
Why she went to prison
And how she lived her life before

Now Lilly mays not stopping
She intends to fill the house
Let's just hope Emmanuel
Don't go back to the Jailhouse

Now talk of Lilly's place
Is just rumours you all know
But Lusha Lee is there
But evidence is slow

So now there's Lilly May
Blondie Cassey Gold
Emmanuel has moved in
Maybe Lusha Lee you never know

So, all eyes on Lilly's house
Let's wait to see who else moves in
Like the Wives of Smalltown said THIS HOUSE IS A SIN.

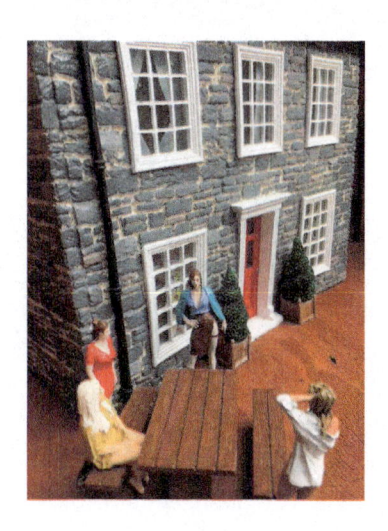

Now Smalltown not very good
There is such a nasty smell
The police they are investigating
They think it's down the Well

Now grandma out for her daily walk
Told council no that's not it
The farmers spreading in the fields
Must be cow's shit

Now the water man very sure
The well we might have to drain
Now grandma shouted really loud
Oh, dear I've got a pain

Oh no my dear old lady
Is the pain in your side
No, it's bloody not
It's in my fat backside

Now she was trying to distract him
Just for a little while
Oh, dear role me on my side
Take the pressure off me piles

Shall I get the doctor
You're making lots of noise
So, would you
If you had Haemorrhoids

Now I'm telling you council man
The well it does not smell
Just as he went to answer her
Off went the lovely Bells

Now you mustn't touch this well
It's been here so very long
So many memories down there
Even if it pongs

That's fine poor old grandma
We will leave it well alone
Now try and stand up
You can Trott off home

So, Grandma's little drama
No draining of the Well for a while
Gran can keep her secret
And get cream for that pile.

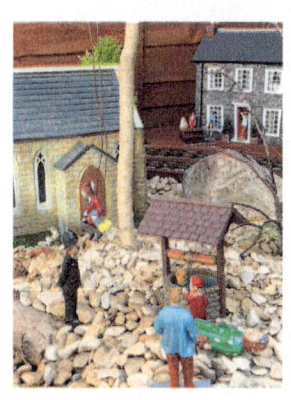

Now reporters will interview everyone
A story for the papers
So cunning Colin and Teresa
Tell us all the capers

Now Teresa sat and told us
Omg what goes on up there
All night long I watch
Men up and down the stairs

Now Colin looked at her-and spoke
It sounds like heaven
But Teresa how do you know all this
You're in bed by seven

Now the reporter asked Colin
Have you ever gone up there
Teresa looked livid
Are you saying he's had an affair

Oh no the reporter said nicely
Calm yourself right down
We're just trying to get a story
Of the ladies in Smalltown

So, the reporters got no information
Or a story as of yet
Smalltown residents kept quiet
In case they say something, they may regret.

Now the Reporters are still busy
The interviews going well
Now there with Alex Albo
Omg he has a story to tell

He started to tell them
That he's been to Lilly mays
Said he had a night up there
But up the chimney he stayed

He tried to be a Jack the lad
And telling a few lies
He quickly shut his mouth
When he heard his Angie's cries

She was fuming with our Alex
Oh, here you go again
Telling all your bloody stories
When will this ever end

Well Angie told the reporters
Up the chimney he got stuck
Don't listen to his stories
He was just covered in soot and muck

Now I know my Alex
And he's pretty tough
If he messed with Lilly
I'd cut his manhood OFF

Reporter said to Alex
Was your time up there really good
Alex told the reporter
No comment, I want to keep my manhood.

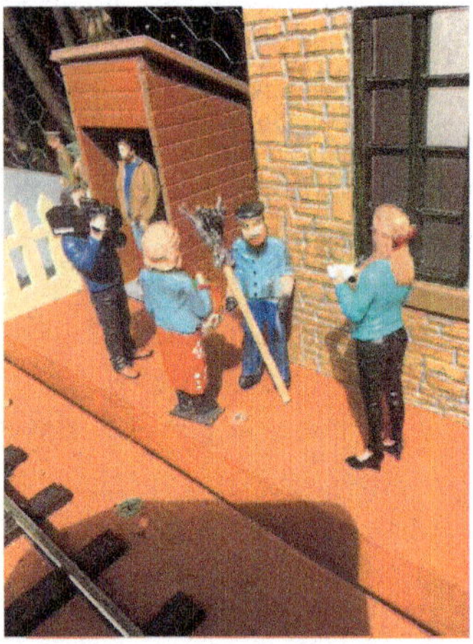

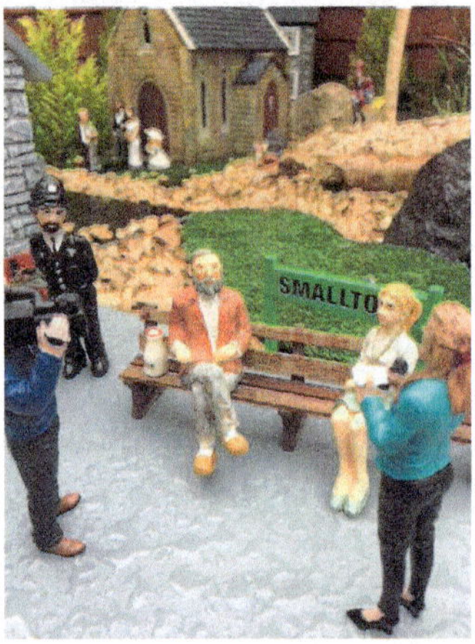
SMALLTO

The reporters they are still around
They want to chat with Lilly May
Residents of Smalltown said
Lilly won't have nothing to say

Now the photographer was very good
Offered a free photo shoot
Just come as you are
I know you can't do swimsuits

Now Lilly chatted to her ladies
Emmanuel said that its great
Cassey gold was happy
But Lusha Lee did hesitate

But today it will be ladies' day
Randy Andy will be out
So will all the other men
So ladies please watch out

Now the method of their madness
Is to find the stories that lie within, of all the ladies
Living in the house of sin

Now they have not found out anything yet
About the ladies of the night
Nothing to go in the papers
So, no story to write

Now the reporter she stood at the door
So many questions she did ask
Hanging on the banister
A beautiful red basque

Now this does not give them any clues
Does not matter what they wear
But the media need a story
Even it's about their underwear

Now Lusha Lee still living there
Now she's really settled in
Perhaps living with Lilly May
Is a new life she'll begin

Now most people in the village
Say it's a house of ill repute
The wives of the village
Say all the women are old boots

But they have not really seen anything
Just men that come and go
The residents of Smalltown
They don't really know

So, Emmanuel and Cassey gold
Lusha Lee and Lilly May
They are fantastic characters, so Smalltown they will stay.

Fishing Phil has got a new Rod
Plan a trip to Norway to catch cod
Lockdown has not gone down so swell
He decided to fish in Smalltown well

So, what's in the end of his hook
We need to go and have a look
He pulled it up it landed on his belly
OMG a smelly welly

Now is this what is making the smell
Maybe no body down the Well
Now Phil he put his line back in
He then pulled up a bottle of Gin

Now this became a game to play
Wishful thinking, he could pull Lilly May
So, in the line went
Phil started to dance
Next that came up a pair of pants

Everything that came up looked quite shoddy
Omg what if there is a body
Walking up came policeman Bob
Hello Phil you catching cod

Phil my friend I need to pick your brains
Have you pulled up human remains Poor ole
Phil didn't know what to say
So just said to Bob um not today

Fishing Phil packed up his fishing gear
The thought of a dead body made him feel queer
Now Bob he shouted are you feeling sick

Don't worry Phil I'm taking the mick

Poor old Phil he looked so pale
A body could be the awful smell
So was there a murder
A body down the well

Only Grandma knows
Only time will tell.

Smalltown has its own Tea Bar
Visitors come from near and far
Now it's been put up next door to The Mill
Buy one tea and get free refill

Now the Mill they have a tea break
Start your morning with a breakfast bake
Now their break is only 10 small minutes
So, the tea bar just one quick visit

Now visit the Snack shack on your lunch
They do a great dinner brunch
There's always a great big que
The shack has some great reviews

Saturday's great beans on toast
Sunday fantastic Roast
Victoria sandwich free cup of tea
Or Eccles cakes and coffee free

Now the General Stores he supplies the stock
Everything she orders always in stock
The lady who runs it you all have seen
It's our Jolly Jean, the drag queen

As we all know she is a man
She always has been since her life began
Now the vicars secret he still keeps
Managed to keep it a secret for weeks

But he will be so very tired
Running the cafe and church choir, so we will
wait for his story to be told
Just watch this space as his life unfolds

Now bedtime he's completely knackered,
Running two lives he must be shattered, Sunday
service they sang lovely songs,
But the vicar left his eyelashes on

Lilly May gave the vicar a wink
The vicar knows what Lilly May thinks
She whispered to the vicar you know what's best
You definitely look better in a DRESS.

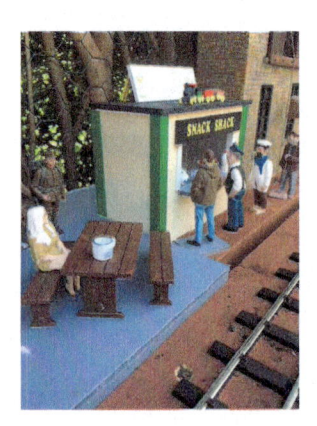

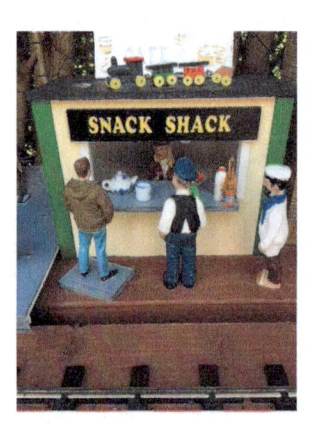

Bikers they have moved into Smalltown
Gran shouts "the towns out of control
Poor Frank comes running out
There into Sex and Rock n Roll

Now a biker lady sat there
Looking stunning on her bike
Along came STIG
A biker lady he really likes

Now Grandma she was panicking
Oh my god they will run us out of town
Now juicy Janice the biker said
OMG calm yourself down

My name is Juicy Janice
I've introduced myself to Stan
Now we are not causing trouble
And yes, we are a Biker gang

Her friend he was in the pub
He's setting up a deal, in a few weeks
All will be revealed

Now Alex he came out the door
Shouted loudly out to Ang
Angie come here quickly
There are 100 bikers in a gang

Now Angie looked out the window
Alex you're really full of it
Alex said but there's 100 bikers
Oh, Alex will you stop talking shit

Now in a few weeks
Bikers moving in
Biker could take over
And use the house of sin

Now Stan he told Juicy Janice
I've always been a leader of the pack
I rode 500 miles
With a kitten on my back

Well Juicy Janice sat there
looking at our Little Stan
He said well any problems with your bike
I'm definitely your man

Now gran she was hysterical
Running in and out the shops
Shouting very loudly
Someone fetch the cops

Janice started laughing
Still waiting for her mate
Told some of Smalltown residents
We are still waiting for a date

Now Smalltown has a house of sin
A place where all men go
And now a town of bikers
Sex, Drugs and Rock 'n' Roll.

45

Great news for today
The pub has opened up the doors
It will not be the same
As you have to follow rules

You will sit at the table
And there you will stay
Served by Lilly
Who's helping out for the day

John he was in there
He was stood near to Lilly May
Mavis shouts to her
Watch him, he will have his evil way

Alex was sat with Angie
Think there will be a pub bash
Angie replied to Alex
Hear it's all about a rash

Mavis wasn't stopping
Wanted to get John really mad
Shouted for everyone to hear
You were the worst I ever had

Mavis shouted again
Well John I'm having your baby
Mavis what you on about
You are one crazy lady

You're telling all your stories
Coming out with all your lies
It would be a bloody miracle
You're knocking on 65

Mavis stop talking rubbish
You wouldn't let me in
And to be honest
I was put off by your hairy chin

The landlady she shouted
Mavis and John enough is enough
Go collect all your belongings
Now leave with all your stuff

Apart from Mavis and John
Causing Merry hell
The opening of the pub
Went really well.

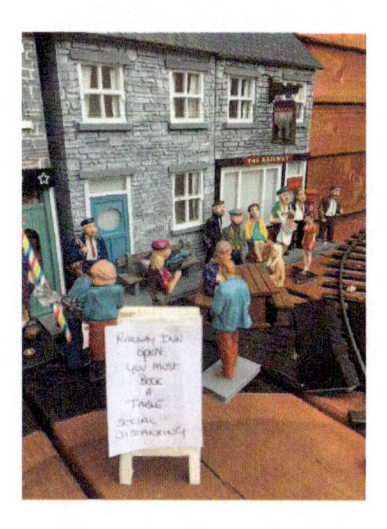

The Carpenters have turned up
They're fitting some new floors
The last time the chippies were here
They forgot to fit the doors

Nice couple of chaps
Steve and Aaron, a great team
Aaron was doing some work
Then Steve heard him really scream

He'd picked up a hammer
Threw it at poor Stan
Lucky for Stan the man
He caught it in his hand

Steve, he stood there
OMG Aaron what the hell
You could have hit him in the head
He could have had a massive swell

Steve was working really hard
Trying to fit a door
Customer was not happy
Said it looked a bloody eyesore"

Steve was fuming
Caused a massive rut
Customer was perfectly right
The door it wouldn't shut

Well Steve he got quite snotty
He slammed the door real hard
The poor customer behind it
Flew out across the yard

Well, I'm telling you Steve and Aaron
Worst carpenters I've ever had
The feedback that I will give you
Is going to be really bad

Well Steve he looked at Aaron
Oh well this job we didn't pass
Well, I'll just take his door
And shove it up his arse

Aaron said I'm off to the pub
Steve said well do what you like
Aaron packed his kit away
Steve he just rode off on his bike.

Quiet Timothy a lovely lad
He lives with his mum
She's never let him go
He is her only son

She watches his every move
Won't let him out her sight
He could never go near
The ladies of the night

Well, his mum went to Newtown
Timothy was getting led astray
Someone took a fancy to him
Our lovely Lilly May

Now Timothy services the oil tanks
Lilly May asked him if he's free
Timothy, I need a little oil
Would you like to service me

Well Timothy he stood there
Said, I think I see me mum
Lilly said you're going nowhere
The only thing you'll see is my little bum

Timothy didn't know where to look
The signal box will go inside
Hurry up in Lilly
We really need to hide

Lilly said Timothy
Let's hide behind the tank
Chase me really quickly
My bottom you could spank

Timothy looked around
No sign of his mother anywhere
Come on Timothy chase me
I'm not wearing underwear

Poor Timothy a lovely chap
Sits in evenings with his mother
Now he has the chance
To have a secret lover

Now Lilly May loves a challenge
Timothy, she wants to have ago
Will she get her way with him
Only Timothy really knows

They ran up the stairs
To the signal box
Looking for fun within
The bloody door was locked

Well Timothy got so excited
And a little scared
Lost his footing completely
Fell right down the stairs

He led there unconscious
Lilly May couldn't bring him round
All she could hear
Was his mum in the background

Well, his mother she got to him
Timothy now what did I say
Stay away from these women
They'll lead you a bloody stray

Well Lilly looked straight at her
Timothy needs some real good fun
He needs a night out with a good woman
And not stuck in with his mum.

The hairdressers have opened
Make sure you book a date
A smashing job always done
Hairdressers Karen and Kate

Safety measures very good
All put into place
So go to boutique Hair and beauty
The staff will keep you safe

They make you very welcome
Great hairstyles for everyone
You'll leave the Hairdressers
With a job well done

Now mistakes they can happen
A new tap Kate had installed
Customers head got stuck on it
A massive patch was bald

Kate tried to cover it up
It was right in the back of her head
Karen said to Kate
Shall I colour it in in red

The bald patch she won't notice
It's on the other side
Unless her eyes in the back of her head
This patch I know we can hide

Kate, she kept very quiet
The customer went to pay the bill
Kate said, this ones on the house
The customer said that's brill

The customer left happy
Can't charge her, no we can't
Karen said, we were lucky
Kate said, I nearly peed me pants

Well Karen if she comes back
Tell her it was fine when she left
deny all knowledge
Whatever happens don't confess

Kate, she had another customer
Best hair you ever seen
Kate has a stressful day
Turned her hair so very green

Kate, she tried to explain
It's a beautiful shade of green
Karen said you having a laugh
It's the worse I've ever seen

I look like a golf course
All that's missing is the balls
Well Kate told the customer
Well, I think your being cruel

Karen said to the customer
I'd like hair the colour of grass
Well Kate she looked at Karen
Oh Karen, stop talking out your arse

Although some mistakes have happened
Boutique hair and beauty great place to be
They do a fabulous job
And make a smashing cup of tea.

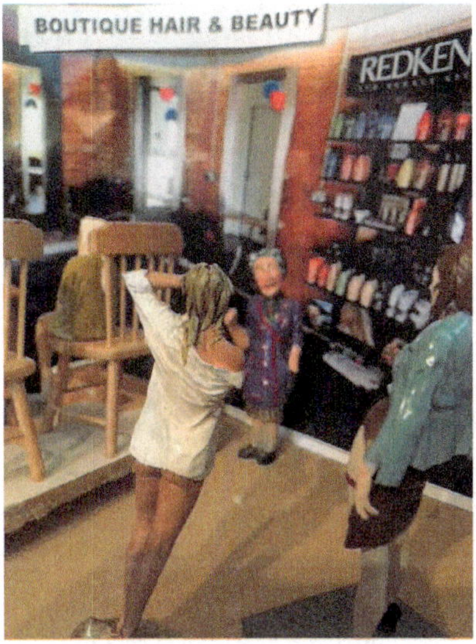
BOUTIQUE HAIR & BEAUTY
REDKEN

Randy Andy got a new tractor
Said to Doris my best ride
Well Doris looked at him
Like she was going to cry

Well Andy, you always told me
I was the best ride you ever had
Now you're in love with your Tractor
Now that makes me sad

Oh no my little Doris
This Tractor won't be rocking
You're the only one for me
Let's keep the bed post rocking

Doris hop up on the Tractor
I'll take you for a ride
Well, that made Doris happy
The tears she couldn't hide

Now why he wants a Tractor
Doris does not really know
They only have some tiny land
And nowhere else to go

But you know what men are like
They love their big boys' toys
Doris shouted, omg turn it off
I can't stick that bloody noise

Well, the engine sounded knackered
And really bloody loud
Loads of residents turned up
The noise it brought in quite a crowd

Black smoke flew out the engine
Steam shot out from everywhere
The chap that sold it to him
Said it's fine, just wear and tear

Doris said how much did it cost you
A lot, now don't be mad
Well Andy you're a foolish man
I think that you've have been had

Well Andy put his foot down
Something shot out the back
Hit poor Stan in the head
He was led out in the track

Now Doris she was fuming
Andy, you have bought a load of shit
I'll be back in an hour
So, you best get rid of it

Well Andy he was feeling sad
A Tractor was his dream
But perhaps Doris is very right
Andy took it to the extreme

Andy looked at his Tractor
My poor Tractor it is dead
He took a deep breath in
Headed back to their shed

Now Doris she was saddened
Said it really is quite shocking
Put her arms around Randy Andy
Come on, let's get the bed posts knocking

So, the moral of this story
Is to stick with what you know
Or you could buy a Tractor
That really does not go.

Graham was out cycling
Dressed in his Lycra gear
Had his helmet on his head
Covering up his ears

Everyone that spoke to him
Shouted move out of the way
Graham didn't hear nothing
Just smiled, and said have a lovely day

He was flying around Smalltown
Cycling really fast
The residents shouted
Slow day you'll cause a crash

Graham decided
It would be great to race the train
His Foot fell off the pedal
His manhood in so much pain

He got off his bike
And his under bits were sore
Rang his wife Julia
And said, I'm not cycling anymore

Julia I'm coming home
I got the worse pain ever
Oh, dear my poor Graham
Come home I'll kiss it better

Graham, walked up the garden
Julia said you look in lots of pain
All his Lycra damaged
Honest Julia, I'm never cycling again

He sat on the Sofa
Checked in on his Strava
It's all good Julia
I had the best time ever

Well Julia just looks at him
And said, you and that bloody bike
Fall off it one more time
I'll do something to it you won't like

Julia don't worry
I promise this will be the last time
Sit down put your feet up
Let me fill your glass with wine.

Now Smalltown have a Milkman
He milks all his own cows
He's a very clever chap
Very good with all the know-how

Now he gets up really early
To deliver pints of milk
Drops a pint at Lilly mays
Great seeing her in her silks

Now she's always up very early
And greets him at the door
Invites him in for a cuppa
And a whole lot more

Well, he sits there very quiet
Really not much to say
Just can't take his eyes of Lilly
Another man in love with Lilly May

Now on Monday he gives her 2 pints
On Wednesday she then has three
On Friday he takes another pint
To cover all his tea

After Lilly's he's off to the cleaner
But she's really full of it
Telling the milkman
About her personal itch

Well, the milkman he's not sure what to do
Does not know what he should say
Told her he does not want a cuppa
I've just had one at Lilly's Mays

Omg that little Trollop
She always gets in first
Have your ruddy milk back
I want to be reimbursed

I'm sorry little Mavis
I don't know what to say
Well, I'm not being second best
When you've been up there with Lilly May

Well, the milkman he stood quiet
For 5 minutes he did pause
Ah I know what it is with her
It's that bloody menopause

Well, the Milkman knew she wasn't right
Mavis, sorry you felt mislead
Your head scarf is on the back of your chair
And you're wearing your knickers on your head.

Steve and Aaron at the Mill
And jobs need to be done
They had been there hours
Before any work begun

Now Aaron was checking the decking
On top of it sits a big machine
Aaron fell on the button
The biggest mess you'd ever seen

He was covered right up to his neck
What looked like cows' manure
Well Steve he stood there laughing
Aaron said, bloody hell I fell through the floor

Steve, he grabbed a rope
Aaron hold it tight
Well Aaron just fell backwards
Steve just said "OH SHITE."

The Manager came over
What's going on here lads
Steve said very quickly
That decking was really bad

Oh dear, the Manager looked at Steve
Well, is your little friend alright
I don't have a clue
He fell from such a height

Well, the manager quite concerned
Let's get the doctor to your friend
As for the decking Steve
It needs to be condemned

Now they were having a good chat
Aaron still stuck in shite
Don't worry about me
I think I'll be alright

Steve, he got a ladder
Oh, Aaron you look quite pale
Of course, I do you're a silly SOD
It was dangerous when I fell

Steve handed Aaron a hammer
Come on then, chop chop
When you were down there
All our work came to a stop

Well thanks for all your help, Steve
You do know I could have died
Oh, come on Aaron
I just think you've hurt your pride

Aaron, he stood there
With huge hammer in his hand
All of a sudden Steve screamed
God knows where that hammer did land.

A beautiful day in Smalltown
Residents enjoying the day
Out comes the Hot tub,
In goes Lilly May

The Hot Tub is for everyone
They all pay their bit
But Lilly and her Ladies
Seem to have the run of it

Now the women of the village
They get a little mad
The men of the village,
Best view they have ever had

Lilly, she lays there
Her day is quite Devine
Watching the world go by
And drinking lots of wine

The men hide behind the bushes
Trying to get a good look
When Stan turns up with fishing rod
In the Hot tub drops a hook

Lilly she was fuming
OMG you stupid fart
What you trying to catch
Well, it would be nice to catch a Tart

Lilly she just looked at him,
Right now, I'll have my say
Never ever come to my house
With me you'll never play

Now Stan he felt a little silly
I've got me self it a rut
I'm very sorry Lilly
I should have kept my big mouth shut.

Smalltown have a lollipop lady
She'll get you across the track
But she won't hang around
You'll have to get your own self back

She said her job is not good
And really lousy pay
So that's why she goes home early
And only sees you across one way

The other day Randy Andy
Was Waiting for hours
Carol shouted across the track
Alright my little flower

Andy shouted at her
I want to get across the track
Well, I don't get paid enough
To bring you all the way back

Now the rules in Smalltown
You must not cross the track on your own
But that does not help
When carol has gone home

Well Carol she was playing up
And still Moaning about her pay
Until you put them up
Then I'll only cross them one way

Well, the Manager of Carol
Said Carol you are taking this to far
Well, if you upset me
I'll take you to HR

Most of the Residents
They have really had enough
They say trying to get back to Smalltown
Carols making it real tough

Lilly shouted to Carol
Carol replied I really don't care
Lilly just stood waiting
Carol said, I'm off to do me hair

Lucky for Lilly May
She was on the side of the signal box
Bob was sat in there
When his door it went knock knock

Bob, he tried to unlock the door
There stood Lilly May
Well Bob he smiled from cheek to cheek
Omg lucky me, Lilly you've made my day.

Everything seemed quiet
No shouting in Smalltown
Just past 12 o'clock
All hell was going down

The Mods they all turned up
The bikers they got tough
Mavis was being nosey
As the night got pretty Rough

Well Graham he turned up
In his cycling gear
Said come on you lot
What's going on here

Well two of the bikers
Pulled each other's hair
One of the MODS
Whacked a biker with a chair

Lots of things got broken
Tables, glasses and the chairs
Still 2 bikers fighting
And still pulling each other's hair

Well, the warriors were not beaten
The bikers they did win
Janice shouted you Mods have lost the battle
Take it on the chin

Well, the residents of Smalltown
Said omg what a night
They never seen this happen
In Smalltown such a fight

Well Mavis, she loved it
Told Frank I'll get myself a bike
Dressing in leather
This I think I'll like

The Mods they left Smalltown
But a scooter left behind
Janice put it in her shed
I'll deal with it, when I'm in a better frame of mind

The Mods they were not happy
Their off to join another pack
I don't think it will be long
And the Mods they will be back.

Reporters have come to Smalltown
They heard about the fights
This crazy little village
And what went on at night

Well Alex was the first
Alex what did you see
Well, this biker grabbed me
So, I gave him me knee

I got him in a headlock
Dragged him to the floor
This big muscly biker
Won't mess with me anymore

Angie, she stood there
Alex you were in the bath
You did not hear a ruddy thing
Stop being bloody daft

You didn't come out
You didn't have a fight
Omg my Alex
What are you like

Well, the vicar he was next
Vicar what went wrong
Well, the biker he came after me
But ran when he seen me thong

Next interview was Mavis
What biker did you catch
I kicked a MOD in the goolies
Now I'll get me biker's patch

Now Janice they interviewed
I'm the landlady of the pub
Only Residents and bikers
No MODS in my nightclub

Stan the man came storming in
I took on all the biker bunch
Everyone laid on the floor
When I laid them all a hefty punch

Well, it seems Smalltown handled this
Lots of tough residents around
So, if the MODS come back
They'll be chased back out of town

Well, they had a chat with Frank
He said they trampled on me plants
Well did you fight them off frank
No, I ran, I shit me pants

Well, the reporters had their story
Smalltown handled this so well
The night the MODS came to Smalltown
Then ran off like Merry hell.

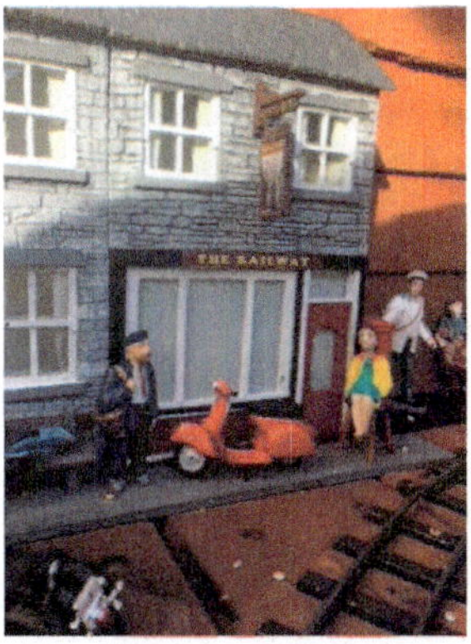

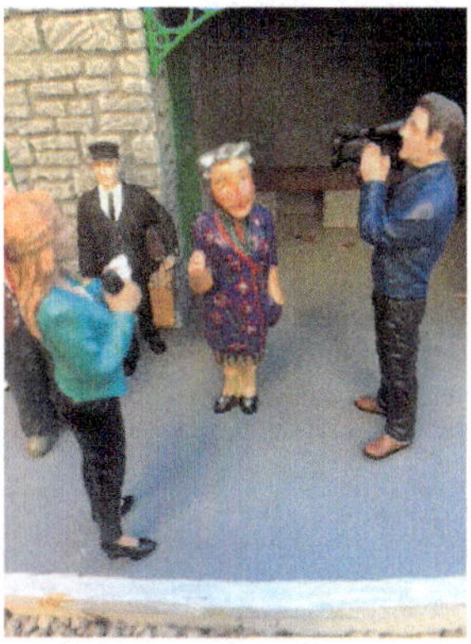

Mavis was shopping in Smalltown
She went to the general stores
Tripped as she came out
Hit Frank to the floor

Frank, he led there
Flat out on his back
Omg Mavis I fell
And something it went crack

Lilly, she came down
With Mavis tried to get Frank up
He was far too heavy
So, they both give up

Just at that moment
The vet came through the door
What happened here
And why are you on the floor

It was all fine
Mavis ran out the door
Hit me really hard
I fell to the floor

Have you called the doctor
Or maybe an ambulance crew
We have not called anyone
But you're a vet so you will do

The vet said I'll try
He put a long glove on his arm
Omg I'm not a cow
You could do me real harm

Omg Frank I'm sorry
I nearly forgot myself right now
I've been up to the farm
Just examined a pregnant cow

Poor ole Frank shocked
His eyes nearly popped out his head
The vet looked at him
Frank I'm glad you quickly said

Well Mavis she was in stitches
Frank well that would have been a surprise
If he had not stopped
He would have brought water to your eyes

Frank, he shouted at her
Stop laughing get out my shop
This is all your fault
And don't forget your mop

The vet examined Frank
Well, I think you are quite fine
Just rest up for a while
And please call your doctor next time.

There's a Shoplifter in Smalltown
They rode off on a stolen bike
Charlie had it on display
One everybody liked

Now Graham wanted to purchase it
A deposit he had paid
Now he's disappointed
As getting it will be delayed

The craft shop things were stolen
Loads of balls of wool
Nobody seen anything
No one seen anything at all

Now Franks little shop
A stock take had been done
Now he's found out
He's another one

All the baked beans taken
He's shocked over 30 tins
100 black bags
And a Small recycling bin

The police have been called
Finger prints they want to take
There's definitely been a thief
Of that there's no mistake

Now who would pinch in Smalltown
We really are quite shocked
The naughty shoplifter
Has just run a mock

The police said were looking for a person
Who might be selling bike parts
He could be wearing a brand-new knitted jumper
And suffer bad with the farts.

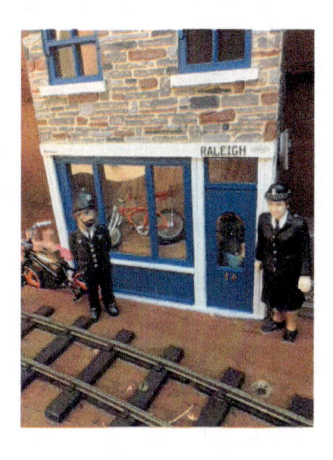

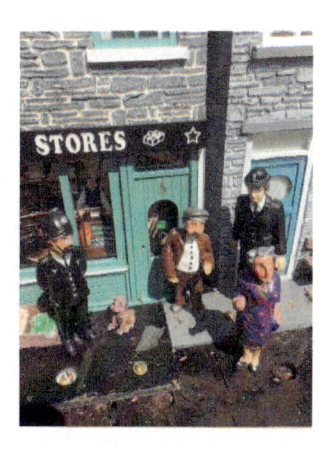

Now Tracy's has called a meeting
Team leader needs a word
We've had complaints about the toilets
And it really is absurd.

Now Kev said there's a problem
Someone's not flushing the loo
We come in every morning
And greeted by huge poo

Well Roxanne said it's terrible
I do the best I can
But whoever it is
They need to eat more bran

Now Tracy said we will sort this out
We will spy on who goes in
Check the toilet after them
Now make sure you hide behind the bin

Well Louise she spent the morning
Running in and out the loo
The phantom toilet messer
Had not left a poo

Just as Louise was going
It just turned 10 o'clock
Kev said Louise come back
You really will be shocked

Well Kev he called Tracy
Omg the biggest I've ever seen
Louise she was fuming
Bloody hell that toilet I just cleaned

Shut off the toilet
The cctv camera I will check
We will find the Phantom pooer
This toilet he has wrecked

Tracy checked the footage
Omg it was Johnny Dapper
Kev at last we got him
Smalltown Phantom crapper.

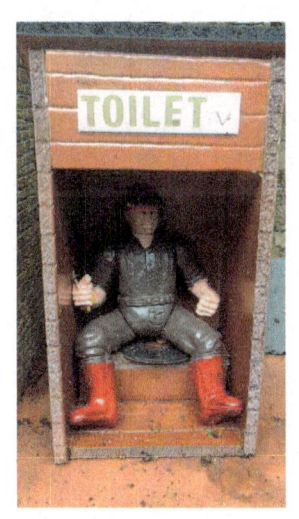

Colin and Teresa
Rode off on some scooter bikes
Well Colin told Teresa
A Proper bike I'd like

Teresa, she looked at Colin
You just want to ride faster
If you had a Harley Davidson
You would be a bloody disaster

Now Teresa she had a surprise
Bought Colin a day van
Now we can go away everywhere
As and when we can

Well Colin said that's brilliant
And that I really like
But Teresa I want to be a biker
And ride a proper motorbike

Well Colin we can go off
Perhaps go to the Isles of Man TT
But don't get your hopes up
A motorbike well wait and see

Colin packed his suitcase
Put it in their day van
Shouted to the neighbours
We are off to the Isle of Man

Led on the back of the seat
Was a brand-new leather jacket
Teresa looked at Colin
That must have cost a packet

A Leather jacket not so good
On a scooter bike
No Teresa I'm coming back
With me Harley Motorbike

Just as they got on the ferry
Colin said I'm excited about the TT
Well thank you Teresa for paying for trip
This Trip is all about me

Well, they had a real great time
But we're driving back really slow
They had a trailer on the back
And a Motorbike in tow.

Pete and Andy, they just rode in
Janice's biker friends
They are running the pub in Smalltown
They are part of Smalltown biker trend

They have been in a biker gang
Andy said her Pete is an old classic
They have always enjoyed the biker life
Wearing leather is just fantastic

Now Andy she loves sitting on the back
The wind blowing in a hair
Oh, Pete he loves his Andy
Said she's a sexy little mare

Now Smalltown it was quiet
Now some loud Motorbikes
But Smalltown residents seem happy
As Stan the Man Owns a classic bike

Now they were good today
Sticking to 6 the COVID Rules
Now they look forward to running the pub
Will not tolerate COVID fools

Smalltown is getting bigger
Now there's a biker pub
They can go to Oldtown
Visit Cod father for some real good grub

The plans for the future
Biker shows every week
Lots of bikes for sale
Bike parts if that's what you seek

Well, everyone excited
Over the moon Stan the man
He said to oh Janice
Smalltown turning into Isle of Man.

Mavis, she plays the piano
But really cannot play
Well Dick he shouted
Shut up or I'll burn that piano one day

Well Mavis she played louder
From her big piano room
She played it for hours
But can only play one tune

Well Lilly May she came out
Mavis, give it a bloody rest
Mavis she again played louder
Alex came out in his string vest

Mavis I'm working nights
And the day has nearly passed
Now shut that ruddy noise
Or I'll shove it up your arse

Mavis slammed the piano top down
Stood on her front door
You all keep moaning
I'll play some ruddy more

Well Angie said to Alex
Your stood out there in your string vest
Now get back in and shut the door
Don't be a nosey pest

Well Dick he knocked on the door
A large hammer in his hand
If you play that one more time
That piano it won't stand

Well Mavis she called the copper
Bob get over here really quick
He's going to smash me piano
No wonder they call you Dick

Bob, he stood there
Quite an argument broke out
Now both of you shut up
Please talk and just don't shout

Well Mavis, she told him
You can't touch it, the pianos mine
Well Dick he said, I WILL
Or I'll shove it where the sun doesn't shine

Well Bob, he told them to stop
No more shouting I must say
Now Dick you go back home
Mavis pack your piano away

Now all went really quiet
Mavis walked away real glum
Don't worry Dick, you didn't win
I've got a set of drums.

A busy day in Smalltown
All the trains out of the yard
The security was watching social distancing
It was left to Everard

Now Mavis she was Moaning
As normal kicking up a fuss
She said that Smalltown
The council should put on a bus

Now the train she has to pay
Said it really is not fair
But if she goes on the bus
She has to pay no fare

Well Mavis she likes a bargain
Better still pay nothing at all
She was getting on the drivers' nerves
Mavis, you're driving me up the wall

Fannies she had a special offer
Fish and chips £3.00 for OAP's
The kids they queued up outside
Can we have them for free

Fannie said get on with you
I'll put you in me batter
Well Jack and his mates shouted
Quick run, she's as mad as a Hatter

It's been a lovely day In Smalltown
All the residents came out
Janice and her biker mates
Loads of visitors about

There seemed a bit of normality
And smiles from everyone
Let's hope in the months ahead
This horrible virus, we have won

Get back with our families
Make up for time that we have lost
But if people still break the rules
Again, it will come at a cost

Let's hope as we look to the future
We will look back at this crazy time
Hug everyone we missed
Knowing now a hug is fine.

Today in Smalltown
Back has come the smell
Granny she was looking worried
The smell is from the Well

The rain it has not stopped all week
The Well has overflowed
The water it keeps coming out
It has nowhere to go

Now why is gran so worried
Why does she stand and stare
She keeps looking down the Well
And she's looking really scared

Now as we said before
Her husband just disappeared
Now the residents of Smalltown
Said it was really weird

Now no search party went looking
Everything seemed undercover
The Gran took in her granddaughter
She knows her as her mother

But where is her late husband
And why does the old lady cry
Why don't the police investigate
We really wonder why

But suspicion in the Town
It's been talked about for years
That she had a husband
Who completely disappeared

Now it really is quite scary
Is there a body down the Well
So many years gone by
Would it still create that smell

Now Halloween tomorrow
Mary she still cries from the lane
Is there some link to the missing husband
And Mary's cries of pain.

Is there some nasty story
Perhaps there is a link
Omg Mary was murdered
Now I definitely need a drink

Now this story is quite crazy
Tales of the unexpected going on here
A murder and a missing person
But soon it will become clear

Well, this all is very interesting
In Smalltown there has been a crime
So, sit on the edge of your seats
All will come out, it's just a matter of time.

So tonight, we know it's a scary night
We all know it's Halloween
Now is someone playing a game
Or someone needs to come clean

Now Smalltown they called off today
Because of covid rules
So is someone messing around
Playing a Halloween fool

Now we all know there's an issue
With the Wishing Well
Now is this the reason
For the Smalltown Smell

No one has notice
A skeleton in the well
Tomorrow what a day
The paper will have hell of a story to tell

So is this grandma's husband
Or a Halloween prank
Tomorrow questions will be asked
How many minds will draw a blank

Now somebody knows something
Of the body in the well
The police will be all over it
Smalltown will be hit with a bombshell

Tales of the unexpected
Maybe Taggart will come to town
Maybe partnered with Vera
An investigation now this body has been found

So good night, everybody
Smalltown is in for a shock
Frank will see the skeleton
As he's up at 6 o'clock

So, all residents of Smalltown
From this mystery they cannot hide
Somebody they know something
Many years ago, in Smalltown, somebody had died.

OMG how weird is Smalltown
The skeleton has disappeared
Now I wonder where he went
Was he taken by the old dear

Now the water board are back again
To get to the bottom of the well
It's definitely getting worse
Making residents feel unwell

No one knows about the skeleton
Nobody has said
The night the skeleton turned up
Was it the night of the living dead

Now detectives are just waiting
To see what the Waterboard fine
Will they come up with nothing
Or will it be the start of a crime

Now Grandma what is she covering up
What does she not want them to see
Now the skeleton has vanished
So did grandma take him back for tea.

Smalltown queueing for the flu jab
Well, the Doctor better be quick
Stan, he said don't worry
It's just a little prick

The receptionist came out
Said to Dr Tamil
Well, I hope this jab
Does not make me ill

You will be fine Steve
Maybe just a runny nose
You should be fine
Hurry up then you can go

Along came Mavis
Pushed in the front of the que
Mavis, you get too the back
Wait for the Doctor to call you

I need to see the Doctor
Someone call Doctor Tamil
Today I got a cough
I'm feeling pretty ill

Omg everyone vanished
Pulled masks up over their Face
One minute there was a que outside
Now no one outside the place

So, Mavis she went in first
Mavis, I understand you're feeling bad
Not at all doctor I'm fine
Just come for my flu jab

Now Mavis she's a nightmare
This time she's played a trick
I hope that karma does not come back
And you end up really sick

Mavis, she headed back
Residents were mad
Mavis you're a wicked woman
What you done was really bad

Well Stan I did nothing wrong
Just said I had a cough
Next minute I looked around
And you lot had all f off.

Christmas trees in Smalltown
Residents have worked really hard
The whole town looks gorgeous
Just like a Christmas card

The Hairdressers they have a lovely tree
Beautiful and real
Christmas offers in there
Katy's doing special deals

Now they had a busy day
Trying to sort out Mrs Hatch
She fell asleep by her rabbit
He ate her hair, now a big bald patch

Now Katy had a furry pencil case
In a nice shade of red
She cut a circle out of it
And stuck it on her head

Well Mrs Hatch seemed pretty pleased
She said that bald patch was such a pain
Well, it looks pretty good
Just a shame about the ink stain

Oh dear, what do you mean?
Karen said it looks fine me old cocker
It's fur of a pencil case
But you look like a punk rocker

Well Mrs Hatch she left
Well got to have fun in our lives
That's right Mrs Hatch
A punk rocker at 85

Well, she headed to the Station
Said her day in Smalltown quite a hoot
Now I'm going into Newtown
To buy myself Dr Martin boots

So, wear what you like
Do it gracefully
If it's Dr Martin boots
That's fine if it makes you happy.

On the 6th day of Christmas
Mr Snowman was missing all day
He told Mary the copper
That he just froze at Lilly Mays

Well Mary she looked at him
Mr Snowman are you for real
Of course, I am just like you
So don't get funny you just chill

Santa, he called over
Get over here I'm going to have ago
You disappeared yesterday
And never packed your snow

I was at Lilly Mays
Started melting over the floor
She grabbed me by me carrot
And chucked me out the door

Well, me long dangly thing
She tore of my big orange nose
She said if I did not get out
Something else would definitely go

Well, I was a little worried
No way risking something else
So, I told her give me my nose back
Or I'm sending in the Elf's

She said if you don't get out
You're a naughty Snowman
I'll lite a big fat fire
And melt you if I can

Now Santa clause I'm just saying
You take Lilly May off the Christmas list
She really frightened me
That Lilly May she's taking the piss

Now Santa Clause is lovely
Quite a cute little geezer
He took home Mr Snowman
And put him in the freezer.

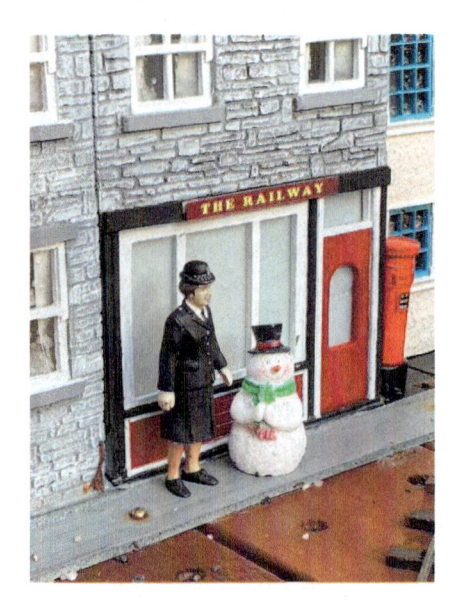

On the 2nd day of Christmas
As soon as darkness fell
Santa was out on his sleigh
He put a pressie down Lilly's chimney
She must have been good today

Santa had a problem
His reindeers nowhere to be seen
But Stan come to the rescue
We can pull you in with steam

He looked through Mavis's window
She was sat talking to little Jack
She said, Santa he won't call to you
So, home you hurry back

Now Frank he's spending Christmas
Stock taking in his shop
He said when you're a business man
On Christmas you don't stop

Well, the Vicar he's not about
Only Jolly Jean
She's dressed up as a fairy
Biggest fairy Smalltown ever seen

Hanging outside Lilly's door
Is mistletoe for residents to kiss
Well virtual hugs only
And a kiss we all will miss

When all the children wake up
They know Santa Clause has been
They will have the biggest Smiles
Residents have ever seen

Goodnight residents of Smalltown
All the children bed early and sleep tight
At 12 o'clock I'll be watching
When it's the Carols at midnight.

A great start to the New year
A good 2021
Poor Mavis she went out last night
This morning, seen by everyone

This morning she was found
In the factory yard
Poor chap still in shock
The security guard Everard

Mavis she was led there
Just in knickers and bra
On her phone was playing
Some great quality music

Omg Mavis what the hell,
You will freeze off all your bits
Mavis still quite drunk
Everard quick cover up me tits

Residents starting gathering
Mavis covered in a sheet
Oh, Happy New year to all of you
And she wobbled down the street

Mavis what were you thinking
Mavis what the Hell
If Bob the copper found you
You could have ended up in jail

Everard I'm fine
Just wanted to say good bye to this year
It's been a hard time for me
Just wanted to see in the New year

I'd just come down from the bath
I opened up the door
The wind it blew
I was stood outside in bra and drawers

Well, I couldn't get back in
And no one was about
Fireworks were going off
No one heard me shout

So, I ran around Smalltown
To keep me warm I sang
Well Mavis your new year
Definitely went off with a bang.

The reporters they turned up
Can we get this story right
Today they printed in the papers
Mavis streaked around Smalltown all night

Mavis said that's wrong
What you've printed in the news
But Mavis said it's quite funny
The first day of the year, Smalltown Residents
were amused

Well, this is just like Mavis
Always in the limelight
Although she said she'd froze her TITs off
Being out there all bloody night.

Stan turned his back for 1 second
What's Mavis up to now
Mavis, you get down
In the steam engine we can't allow

Doris, she told Mavis
There's still the lockdown today
Mavis got quite nasty
Doris, I don't care what you say

Reginald, he got annoyed
Mavis that engine is quite unsafe
If you let the lever go
The Engine it will Race

Well Mavis being Mavis
Ignored everything he had to say
Reginald don't worry
Just 5 minutes I will play

Oh, dear Reginald
I put my hand on the wrong knob
The steam engine it shot forward
Reginald's foot it started to throb

Stan, he looked at Reginald
Omg she's rolled into your foot
Reginald shouted omg
I really don't want to look

Mavis you're a pain
You grabbed the wrong knob
Now Reginald foot is stuck
Someone better get Bob

Bob the copper turned up
Oh, dear now who's to blame
Mavis what are you doing in there
Stan this is insane

Mavis she's caused some trouble
But we need to get his foot out
They moved the engine back slowly
Poor Reginald Passed out

The doctor he came running
Poor Reginald's foot was flat
Stan said to the doctor
Omg take a look at that

The doctor told Reginald
Now everything is fine
Your left foot is size 6
But now your right foot is size 9.

Smalltown woke up this morning
Completely under snow
Frank noticed some snow was moving
Somethings under there you know

Well Stan got his shovel
Just as Alex came out his house
Shhhh, can you hear something
I think it's Mavis's mouth

We thought it was a Snowman
Be careful said ole Stan
He pulled away some snow
OMG there was a hand

It was definitely our Mavis
Up to her neck in snow
I went to get me paper
The kids covered me in snow

Well Alex started laughing
So did ole Frank
Mavis said when I'm out of here
I'll give them kids a spank

Little Jack was hiding
With a yellow snowball in his hand
He threw it really hard
Knocked over poor ole Stan

Frank looked at Stan
That snowball it was rank
I think I better tell you
It was a yellow one said Frank

Well Lilly she was stood there
With her doggy on a lead
Oh, I'm very sorry
Jack took the snow where my dog peed

Poor Mavis she was freezing
She had a bright red nose
She could not even walk
Her body it had froze

Stig, he helped
Stood there with Lilly May
It's a winter wonderland
But Stig had nothing to say

Kev, he got Mavis
A nice hot cup of tea
Oh, Alex my sweet man
Could you run a bath for me

Alex, he went up her stairs
Filled up a real hot bath
Well Alex could you help me
I know it might seem daft

Oh, Mavis what is it
What do you want me to do
I can't really help you
I'm not undressing you

Oh no Frank that's fine
Help me take off my anorak
When I'm in the bath
Do you think you could scrub me back

Mavis, do you realise
There is still a lockdown
The only thing I'll do for you
Is hand you your dressing gown

Alex, he ran like hell
Omg did that man go
He shot out Mavis's door
Landed face down in the Snow

Omg Alex are you ok
Grab my hand hold onto me
You look as white as snow Alex
I think Mavis wanted her evil way with me

Omg Alex I'm shocked
Did she want you to have ago
I think she did Stan
We should have left her in the snow.

Poor Stan he has gone missing
He had his window cleaning gear
Kev said he was up the ladder
Now he's disappeared

The ladder it's left there
Frank said he's not been to the shop
Kev said I've not seen him
And I've been here ages with me mop

Lilly said there's lots of noise
Coming from the shed
Funny Randy Andy's away
I remembered Andy said

Well Kev stood there with Lilly
In the shed was a lot of knocking
Kev said definitely sounds
That the bedpost is a knocking

Well, if Randy Andys not in there
We know he's gone away
Omg Stan is missing
Is Doris playing away

Kev, he said I'll knock the door
There was Doris totally surprised
What's all that knocking Doris
She said, "I'm doing me exercise"

Well Kev he tried to have a peep
Doris tried to shut the door
Is something going on in there
Kev said I'll nose a little more

Kev, he tried but still couldn't see
Well, if she is that's just shocking
Just as Kev and Lilly walked away
The bedstead again it started knocking.

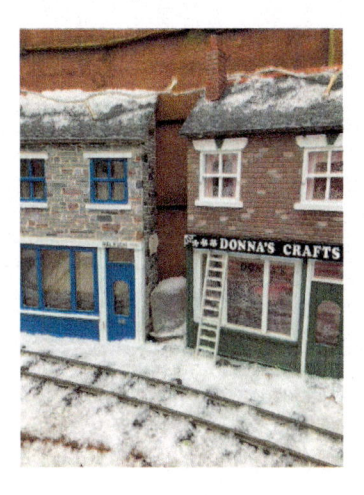

Frank he was talking
Roll on the Summer at the beach
Alex said that seems far away
And might still be out of reach

The ladies they looked stunning
And they brightened up the day
Let's hope we can go there Alex
And Covid's gone away

Frank, he said Remember Mavis
Stood there in her Bathing Suit
Imagine her
In the photo shoot

Seems a long time Alex
But the beach is what we need
Fish and chips and a beer
With that I do agree

All Lilly Mays ladies
The Sandy beach and sun as well
Role on the Summer time
Let's move on from Covid Hell

Frank it's been a nightmare
I miss going to the pub
Me and my lovely Ang
Had just started enjoying the club

Frank and Alex had a good chat
Well, the Vicar I've not seen
Right at that moment
There was Jolly Jean

Good afternoon, Jean
You're looking rather nice
I did not recognise you
I had to look twice

Oh, Frank it's a new lipstick
Bought it from the Avon Book
I am a representative
Would you like to have a look

Alex said to Jean
Drop a book through me door
Angie she might like to look
But I don't wear make-up anymore

Well Frank he looked at Alex
Omg Alex your always acting daft
But you know me Frank
I'm always good for a laugh

Well thanks Frank
Reminiscing over old times
All I can say to you is
Roll on the summer time.

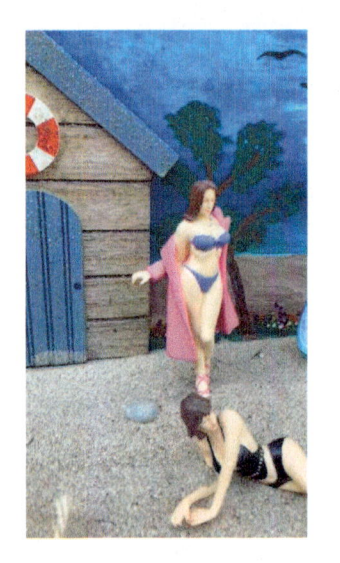

Mavis's sister has arrived
Alex said she's pretty old
He was telling Frank
She's must have come from the same old mould

Mavis she was showing her around
She said Stan looked a little Shady
She didn't like Lilly
She said who's that Tarty lady

She met the Vicar
She said he has no pride
Met men like him before
She said he's got something to hide

She soon met Janice
Outside the local pub
Any late music
And I'll report your club

Next minute there was Alex
Alright then my old cock
Alex said too Angie
Well, she's a chip off the old block

Well, they stood outside the signal box
There was Bob stuck inside
Mabel said to Mavis
Well, he looks good for a ride

Well Mavis she just stood there
Mabel looked at her in vain
Mavis I'm not on about that
I'm mean a ride on a train

Well, it looks like Mavis
Has her sister in her bubble
But I'm afraid poor Smalltown
Now have Double Trouble.

Mabel she's not happy
Said Mavis's house is such a mess
She dragged Mavis to the DIY stores
Mavis is so depressed

Moaning Morris, he runs it
Funny little chap
Does not really smile
Never removes his dirty cap

Well Mabel said she wants everything
The house really could full down
Mavis she just stood there,
On her face a massive frown

Well, she said to Mavis
I want the bigger room
You can have the tiny one
Cheer up, it's not all doom and gloom

Well Mabel she ordered a skip
Throw everything away
Well Mavis said everything
Yes, Mavis nothing needs to stay

Now you need a project manager
Someone has to do the job
You've lived here for many years Mavis
And you've lived like a slob

Alex, he went walking by
Mavis stood with head in hand
Mavis are you ok
No, my sister Mabel has got the upper hand

For the very first time she looked sad
Oh, dear Mavis kick her out
Have you got into an argument with Mabel
You wouldn't win that's no doubt

Well moaning Morris, he stood there
Mabel said I'm after a screw
Poor Morris he went silent
Omg I don't know what to do

Now can I have some nails
And the biggest hammer
Don't forget me screw
And a new screw driver

Morris he went in the stores
Mabel was making quite a fuss
Don't worry Morris
I'm not in any rush

Mavis said to Mabel
That was a little sarcastic
You know he can't really walk
Our Morris is made of plastic

Poor Morris 5 minutes later
Came out with no hesitation
Sorry for the wait
Well, I'm not paying did I forget to mention

Your service is not very good
Mabel got her goods and walked away
Mavis said don't worry Morris
The bill I will pay

Well poor Mavis she just stood there
Sorry Morris she's on another level
She really is Mavis
Your sister is the Devil

Is she married Mavis
If she comes again, I will hide
Well, she's been married 7 times
And every husband they have died

Omg Mavis
That's absolutely shocking
Well, I'm warning you Morris
At your door she will be knocking

She really likes flirting
Can't keep her hands off the men
But all of her husbands
Came to a bitter end

Well looks like Smalltown
Mabel and Mavis, a sister bubble
But the single men in Smalltown
Really could be in some trouble.

The biker gang are fuming
The MODS turned up last night
Mighty Matt said this is not good
They are heading for a fight

Well Mavis said I know them
They come from Brighton Town
Last night I shut the curtains
I seen them hanging around

Now you might want to chat to Stig
He was definitely outside
He came back on a scooter
He'd gone off for a ride

Frank, he came over
We've had trouble with them in the past
But the bikers sorted them all out
Definitely kicked their arse

They said they would come back
None of us knew when
But they said this was not over
They would get their revenge

We still have one of their scooters
Said we'd keep them as a souvenir
We knew they would come back
When all the bikers shouted and cheered

So Smalltown could have some trouble
Another Brighton on our hands
Don't worry said our Mavis
We have our tough man Stan

Well Frank he said to Mavis
Don't you look at me
I don't want any trouble
I'll be shaking in my knees

Their breaking all the rules
Coming to Smalltown
But so are all the bikers
As we are still in a lockdown

Well mighty Matt he's fuming
Well, I'm not taking any of it
Mabel looked at Mavis and spoke
Oh, dear Smalltown in the shit

Well Stan he started to panic
Get some pallets board the windows up
Bring in extra coppers
Smalltown we must shut up

Bob the copper he was there
The bikes all pushed down on the ground
Well, I was out on the beat last night
I never heard a sound

Well, if the Mods think they can come here
Turn our Smalltown into Hell
They will have a nasty shock
I'll throw them all in jail

So today there's extra coppers
Out there on the street
Mighty Matt was stood with Bob-the cop
The Mods I want to meet

CCTV is fully on
Smalltown is very tense
Everyone awaiting
The whole of Smalltown in suspense.

Some exciting news in Smalltown
Lilly May has written a book
Stan Alex and Frank said
We can't wait to have a look

Lilly told them,
Dark secrets are inside
Every story in there
Lilly May has nothing to hide

Frank was telling Mabel
Then she said to Stan
If this book is disgusting
Then I'll fight to get it banned

Well Mabel, I have seen it
I've seen what's on the front cover
This book it is a shocker
Nothing like any other

I'm not very happy
When I see it, I'll have something to say
But I'm celebrating at the moment
I'm an Irish lady and it's St Patrick's Day

Alex said to Frank
I want to get a copy, happy days
The title on the front cover reads
Fifty shades of Lilly May.

So today was rather busy
Don and Daph moved into town
They moved into the cottage
On the outskirts of Smalltown

Well Don he's so happy
That he put his old house up for sale
Little did they know when they moved
Smalltown would be in Garden Rail

Well Don he's so excited
Already got friendly with Stan the man
He's planning his own garden Railway
With some help from Stan

Well Don he's likes to chat
He has told some great stories
But Daphne always tells people
He's a right Jackanory

Now over the coming weeks
So much decorating to do
But Don he said to Daphne
I'll leave that all to you

Don was stood in the garden
Having a good chat with Stan
Now I want to do a garden Rail
So, I'll be showing you me plans

I bought the Magazine
That one called the Garden Rail
Smalltown is famous Daph
And will be living there as well

Well, Daph she said to Don
Well, we are very blessed
Smalltown is going to be lovely
And we can get our well-earned rest

Well Don he looked at Daphne
Well, you speak for yourself
I'm starting my garden Railway
My Train Berties not living on the shelf

Well, that's really great news Don
At least you'll move away from the TV
So, this little garden Railway
I just cannot wait to see

So Daph and Don they will be busy
Tea dancing in the afternoon
Bingo in the evening
They hired the cleaners to clean the room

Well Don he looked at his wife
I really love you my Daph
And I know you don't mean it
When you say, I'm a right pain in the arse.

It's been a lovely day in Smalltown
A beautiful sunny day
All the Residents were doing their gardens
Stan was helping out at Lilly Mays

The shops are getting ready
Working late into the night
All the little premises
All lite up and bright

Now Charlie he's building bikes
Getting ready for hopefully opening time
He's managed to keep his sales up
Selling bikes on line

Now the craft shop that was busy
The wool it sold galore
The manager of the shop
Said she does not have anymore

The sales they said were also good
And again, sold loads on line
It's seeming she done really well
So, her business should be fine

Now the school that is all lite up
Daph and Don having a little glance
Hopefully in 2 weeks
They might start their afternoon Tea and Dance

Well Mabel she came nosing
Stoog outside by the gate
She said she wants to call the bingo
Me and Mavis, two fat ladies 88

There was a lot of banging at Lilly's
She had a hammer in her hand
Down on all fours
Was our Stan the man

Next minute Stan he sat on a chair
Lilly, please give me a hand
I don't have a clue about my census
Don't worry I'll help you poor ole Stan the man

But it's lovely to see Smalltown
Is still alive at night
The residents having Sunday tea
And all the houses shining bright

Now you can imagine what goes on
Behind all the little closed doors
Mavis sat by her fire
In her massive Bridget Jones Drawers

Mabel moaning about everyone
What her plans are for the next day
Stan filling out his census
He's happy, he's with Lilly May

Don and Daph, they are all settled in
But still loads of work to do
Kev he's got an early night
Tomorrow so much cleaning to do

So, goodnight Smalltown
Let's start another week
There's one thing with Smalltown
Life is never bleak.

Dave stopped and spoke to Bob
Said he had trouble with a bin
I picked it up yesterday
Sure, I heard a scream within

I open up the lid
Lots and lots of slime
Just an old pair of black boots stuck up
But everything looked fine

Don't know what the noise was
Could have been a rat
But around the area
A lot of feral cats

Omg said Bob and Mary
Do you think that was Mabel
Who's that said Dave the dustman
The old dear that dances on the table

Where did the bin go
Well, that went to the yard
Everything gets burned
So, to find her would be hard

Oh, dear we need to find Mavis
This is now a crime
It could be old Mabel
She's been missing a long time

Bob, he went to Mavis's
Said to Mary I am trying not to worry
Mavis opened up the door
Oh Bob, about Mabel, don't find her in a hurry

We know that Mabel is a nuisance
And like an old alligator
But we think she was in the wheelie bin
And ended up in the incinerator

Oh, that's terrible
That bin must have really smelled
Thanks for popping by
Now I'm off to watch Emmerdale

Mavis she just shut the door
Omg she didn't even cry
Bob wrote in his notebook
We think Mabel Handcock might have died

Outside in the garden
We're Alex Frank and Stan
Everything alright Bob
Do you need a hand

It's fine lads
But we think Mabel is dead
She went off to the dump
Now she's been incinerated

Alex looked at Frank
Frank, he looked at Stan
Oh, dear I'm shitting me self
Said our Stan the man

Why are you looking worried Alex
Well, it was Stan as well
We've done it now Stan
We'll could be carted off to jail

Alex looked at Frank
Frank, he looked at Stan
This is really serious
We need to come up with a plan

Mavis, she opened up her door
I owe you all a drink
Mavis looked at Alex
And gave him quite a wink

I know that you got rid of her
It's like you all knew I had that wish
Now have yourself a drink on me
And good riddance to old rubbish.

Smalltown are in for a shock
Mabel was buried in the sand
Bob said Mabel has turned up
Mavis said that buggered up me plans

She was washed up on the beach
The kids covered her in sand
Dave the dustman found her
When he just noticed a hand

They quickly said to Bob
We thought it was a whale
It was washed up on the shore line
And she really smelled

Well Bob the copper went to Mavis
Banged loudly on her door
We found your sister Mabel
Oh, dear, are you really sure

She had crawled out the dustbin
Drunken and unsure
She fell into the sea
Lucky for her she washed up on the shore

Well Mavis she looked sad
Shouted over to poor old Stan
They've found oh bloody Mabel
Now that's buggered up me plans

Stan, he ran quickly
Knocked on Alex's door
They've found ole bloody Mabel
Omg are you sure

What if she remembers
That we chucked her in the bin
Our lives will be hell
She'll kick up such a din

But Alex's we were masked up
We had Angie tights on our head
But no matter what
We virtually left Mabel for dead

Next minute there was Mabel
Looking straight at Alex and Stan
Your never guess what happened to me
I was chucked in the bin by a strange man

She did not question Alex
She smiled sweetly at ole Stan
If she starts to remember
Then we need an action plan

Mabel she was stood there
Gazing down the track
The residents of Smalltown
Said the wicked Witch is back.

Don and Daph are arranging
To have a tea dance
Mabel said can we have Dirty Dancing
Daphne said no chance

Stan Might throw you in the air
You'll go through the ceiling
I don't think Mabel
That would be that appealing

Now you can do the Cha Cha Cha
Or maybe a great Tango
Maybe just a slow waltz
Or just a dance with some get up and go

Lilly May she came by
Have you got the rota I liked to have a glance
I really want to learn something
Maybe a footloose dance

We are going to be so busy
Maybe a dance every day
If you want to help
Then by all means Lilly May

Well Mabel she stood there
Looking a little numb
I could do a dance as well
But Mabel, I don't think anyone would come

What dance would you do
What would you teach
Well, I do know the birdy song
That one I could teach

Oh, Mabel I'm not sure
But it might be away to go
Now what about some fast dancing
Like A bit of Rock n Roll

Omg are you out to kill me
That dancing is so fast
Well Stan he said he's up for it
That would be a blast

So, it seems this dancing adventure
We're going to see some dancing feet
The Summer in Smalltown
The Residents are in for quite a treat.

Such a busy day in Smalltown
All the Residents working hard
Randy Andy was enjoying himself
Being the man in charge

All the trains were in Smalltown
Deliveries coming in
Getting ready for the shops to open
When the shoppers can go in

The craft shop it's fully stocked
The bike shop ready for the rush
Frank said I've been open all the time
What's all the fuss

The pub is getting the garden ready
Tables all outside
The train is offering cream teas
And in the train, you can take a Ride

Don and Daph their getting ready
First dance the Cha Cha Cha
Angie said you're learning Alex
Alex said You having a laugh

Well Bob the copper said it's looking good
Lovely a brand-new start
But remember everyone
Still stay 2 metres apart

So, it's all about staying safe
Getting back to reality
Smalltown is looking forward
For the future and hopefully back to normality.

What a great day at the beach today
It really was quite packed
All the lovely ladies,
We're all coming back

Dawn she was there
Looking beautiful at the beach
Agnes was there with Arthur
Making sure the girls were out of reach

Arthur, I'm telling you
Keep that book on your head
I see you look at one of them
I'm telling you you'll be dead

Agnes now come on dear
My eyes are only for you
You're the only woman for me
Now you know that is so true

Little did Agnes know
He could see from under the book
Our naughty little Arthur
Was having a real good look

Well, it's nice to see you smile Arthur
But like I just said
With all these lovely women around
You keep that book firmly on your head.

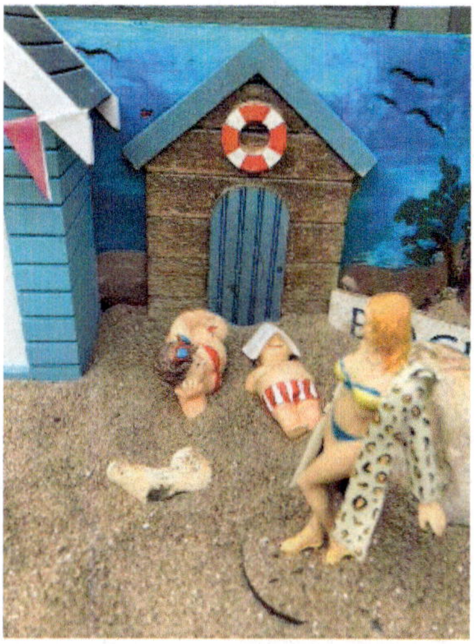

Mabel here she's goes again
She said she's found something out
Now I've got a friend at the council
And she let it all slip out

Now she said up at Lilly's
The grounds having a revamp
Lilly's put in for a licence
To have a nudist camp

Omg said Alex really
Frank a nudist camp he did shout
Well sounds really good to me
The place to go to hang out

Well, I'm not happy about it
Frank and Alex, your acting silly
Well Alex burst out laughing
The place to go to flash your thingy

Now that's enough of that Alex
You just think it's all good fun
Nothing wrong with nudist camps
If your happy to flash your bum

Mabel shouted over to Lilly
The nudist camp Lilly is it true
Of course, it is Mabel
But what's it got to do with you

Well, I'm telling you Lilly
Residents will give you the boot
No, we won't said Frank and Alex
I'm up for walking around in me birthday suit.

Charlie the shop owner
James, are you looking to buy a bike
Well, I'm thinking about it Charlie
A good bike is what I like

Now we have some new ones
Or second hand really good retro
But I heard in the grapevine
Chopper bikes are the way to go

Charlie, you see I need a bike
A new one for my son
And my partner she has told me
I'm only allowed to buy one

You see you can never have enough bikes
And I like a bike or two
Well buy yourself a couple
I mean it's really up to you

Well Jess he said to his daddy
If you buy more mum will get funny
So, you better just buy mine
You don't want to upset Mummy

Jess you are really right
I do have more pushbikes than most
And I'm not too worried
I've got two more coming in the post.

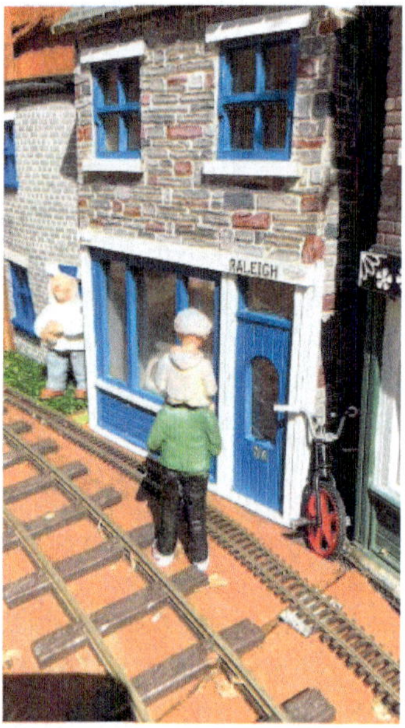
RALEIGH

No trains are running
Off to Tom the Engineer
He said the cracks are a real problem
The repair bills will be very dear

So Smalltown railway out of action
So, Stan he has a plan
He pulled up with a horse and cart
Stan you're a clever man

Well Mabel she just had to be first
Stan shouted" don't get up there now
There were loads of cow's shite
He'd just cleaned out the cows

Well Mabel she couldn't wait
Up to her neck in shit
Well Mabel you wouldn't listen
I told you not too get in it

Mabel she was sat there
Tom the engineer said "you stink
You could only see her eyes
When Mabel had a blink

Tom, he started laughing
I'll clean her with the hose pipe
He did not turn the pressure down
Poor Mabel she took flight

Alex he was watching
He was laughing his head off
Frank he couldn't stop laughing
But made out he had a cough

Mabel, she came flying down
Landed on her back
She only landed on top of the train
So now it definitely has a crack

To everyone's surprise
Mabel stood up and said oh wow
Alex looked at Frank and spoke
Let's hope she listens to Stan now

So, everything turned out ok
Tom the Engineer has a job to do
But Mabel she still really stank
Still head to toe in poo.

Don and Daph they have been busy
Tidying up the yard
But they got a little tired
Found it a little hard

So, Jack and Jill they came over
We can help you if you like
Jack said he's saving money
For a brand-new bike

Daphne said that's fine by us
We will pay you for your time
Then you can get your new bike
You'll buy it in no time

Jill she was stood there
Well Flip Flop he came in
He was quacking really loud
Making such a din

Next minute there was Steve
Flip flop you get home
He's out of control this duck
Always on the roam

Jill said can I play with him
I'll bring him back today
Of course, you can that's fine
If he does not fly away

Jack and Jill, they cleaned the yard
Help Don plant his runner beans
Don said it's just perfect
Best garden I've ever seen

Daph said this is great
I've sat here and had a rest
I like Jack and Jill visiting
It really is the best

So off Jack and Jill went
Daph handed them some money
Jack said that it's brilliant
Daph said "Well your very welcome Sonny."

Beautiful evening in Smalltown
The new train out on the track
Janice was really happy
The pub it was quite packed

Ant he's settled in quite well
Offered a train ride for free
The snack shack offered a burger
Buy one, get one free

The pub is open very late
Lilly's girls behind the bar
Ant, he said it's brilliant here
Some people are quite bazaar

Frank Stan and Alex said
You could be in our Smalltown gang
We like a drink some gossip
And when we're drunk, we really hang

Well, I'm up for that said Ant
I'm so glad I left my wife
Smalltown is just brilliant
It's gave me a whole new life

The women they are stunning
I'm mean look at Lilly Mays
The nudist camp is perfect
I had my clothes off all the day

Janice, she loves her pub
And I'm enjoying the lock ins
It really is just the best
When were all drinking within

Now Bob the copper he's just great
He's definitely turning a blind eye
Frank was park on double yellow lines
Bob the copper he just walked by

I've really settled in
Smalltown is just fantastic
A crazy little village,
Where the people are made of plastic.

Mavis she is fuming,
She went in her garden for a pick
Omg she shouted
My Runner beans they've all been nicked

She went out with her basket
To pick her runner beans
I'll check out the camera
See if anyone was seen.

Mavis and Stan were checking
When Mavis said I feel sick
The thief was on the camera
Sister Mabel is the one who nicked

She was at the General store
Mavis said I can't believe what I've just seen
That ruddy sister of mine
Is selling Frank my runner beans.

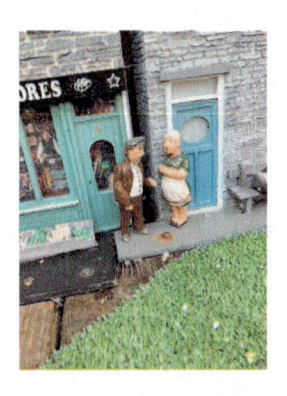

It is that time of year again
Smalltown put on a bike show
Stan is there with his chopper bike
They say it's the best place to go

The fun will start early
Selling around the tents
When the weekends over
You'll be so glad that you went

Now Stan he's got his chopper bike
He has it ready just in time
He's entered his big chopper in
For the show and shine

It's brilliant what you see
Grown men on chopper bikes
Mavis she is going
"I'll sit on Stans chopper that's what I like,"

Now Mavis she's got really into it
But has not ridden one for a while
She's waiting for the doctor
To check on that bloody pile

The show is filling right up
At the pub plenty of beer
Make sure you take plenty of money
To buy your biker gear

They done a great big raffle
Mavis was so surprised
Stan, he offered Mavis up
She was going to be first prize

Well Stan, he said it funny
Nobody wanted to buy
That really is very strange
I really wonder why

That's not really the best way
Now they would sell plenty
If first prize was Lilly May

So, if you want a day out
Go to the Retro Rally
Walk down past the hairdressers
Turned left just at the alley

There you will see lots of men
Sat on their pride and joys
Loads of chopper bikes
And grown men with their big boys' toys.

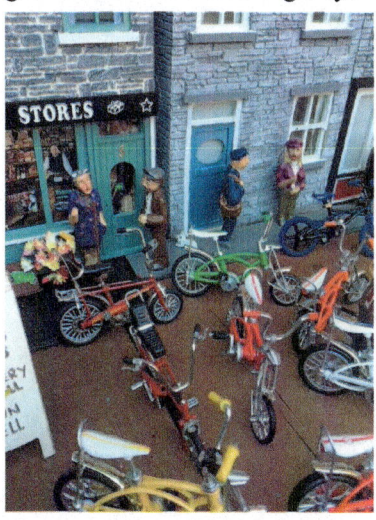

Do you remember Don
The memories gone by
Things have moved on so much
In just a blink of an eye

The children were out playing
Riding on their bikes
The laughter was amazing
And not a phone in sight

I remember on a Sunday
Sat down on my arse
It took me hours
To clean all me brass

I remember the street party's
Omg fancy dress it was so daft
But all the neighbours got together
We all had such a laugh

Do you remember Don
The key hanging behind the doors
Sad now in this day
That does not happen anymore

Do you remember Dawn
She'd turn a head or two
Stunning young lady
So very pretty too

Remember Mr Pitman
Omg his ferrets made me run
He put one in my hand
The little bugger bit me thumb

He laughed so much he couldn't stop
He fell right off his stool
I remember going home
I was Feeling quite the fool

But it healed very quickly
There was no scar that you could see
Amazing what that stuff does
The brilliant TCP

I remember the bonfires
The kids built so very high
Then the gang from the other village
Burned them down, the flames right up in the sky

But the kids they built it up again
On bonfire night the kids galore
They put their bake potatoes in them
Does that happen anymore

Do you remember the silver jubilee
Oh, we had such a ball
A fabulous street party
So much fun for all

Don, do you remember all the dogs
All loose and we didn't know what to do
I remember the kids coming in
They walked in White dog poo

I remember going to the butchers
Getting tripe and onion for my dad

Don't think I could eat that now
Back then, best meal you ever had

I remember watching me dad
In his little flat cap
Cleaning out the aviary
My dad, amazing lovely chap

I remember the coal man
Carrying the coal on his back
Do you remember the coal man Don
Covered in coal completely black

Back then they were good old days
Back then I think we had it right
Wasn't it lovely Don
Like I said before, not a phone insight

I remember the school holidays
A day at the park with a packed lunch
You knew the kids were safe
They all went off in quite a bunch

Some days Don
I'd like to turn back the clock
Some days I sit listen
And hear the clock
Loudly go Tick Tock

But that was the good old days
Now I look at our future plans
Don't you worry about the future Don
I've got it all in hand

As Don and Daph sat reminiscing
Daph I've really had a great life
I've been a very lucky man
Because I've had you for my wife

The day it past so quickly
But they had enjoyed their lovely chat
Talking of the good old days
Don it's lovely to look back.

Well, Smalltown is trimming up,
Ready for Christmas cheer,
Mavis was up early this morning,
Alex said "look at her nosey ole dear."

Everyone has got together
A busy day ahead
Janice has put on some snacks
And the beer straight to Franks poor head

It's such an atmosphere
And everyone so merry
But then the Vicar said
I think that could be the Sherry

Mavis, she made cress sandwiches
Angie the sausage rolls
Doris, she made a nice cheese flan
Lilly May some nice coco

Everyone working so hard,
Santa's grotto will be such fun
Mavis said she'll sit on his lap
As it's open to everyone

The council gave the money
Good cheer to one and all
They said Smalltown this year
Can have themselves a ball

Lilly she was stood there
Putting up some mistletoe
When Mavis grabbed poor Stanley
And said "Come here let's have ago."

Just at that moment
The Church bells were rung
Poor Stanley was nearly sick
"OMG bloody Mavis used her tongue".

Next minute Mavis looked at Alex
"Go on Alex get in the queue
After I've finished with Frank
I'll be french kissing you."

Poor Men of smalltown
Throwing up still our Stan
Well Angie shouted at Mavis
"Keep your hands off my man"

Well Alex looked at Stan,
"My Ang she's gunna smack her."
When Mavis shouted to Alex,
"Come on Alex I'll be your Christmas cracker."

Next minute there's was Angie
With a cheese flan in her hand
She threw it at Mavis
It missed and hit poor Stan

Bob the copper he came over
"This must stop I insist
If you don't stop it now
You're all on the naughty list."

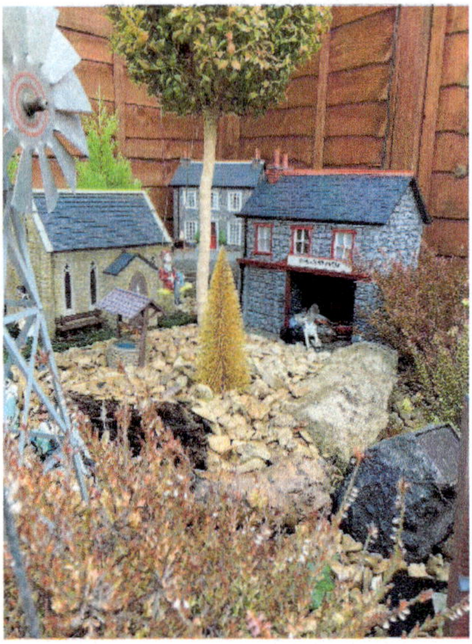

About the Railway

Glebe Valley Railway is a garden railway that is a 16mm scale with live steam locos and some electric locos.

It is based on a narrow-gauge railway, the track is 32mm. It started in 2019 and gradually built-up overtime.

There is an article with more information about the railway in the Garden Rail magazine, April 2021, issue 320 edition.

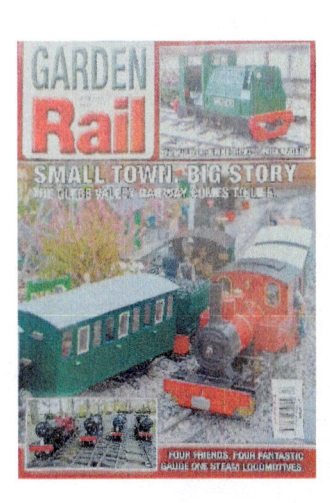

About the Author

Donna Mitchell was born in Bath, England, where she continues to live with her husband. Together, they have two children and four grandchildren. Donna has always loved poetry and decided to write some humorous poems about the characters living in her garden railway. It started off as some entertainment for family and friends during the lockdown period, but she has kept going since people have told her how much they love it.

When not writing her poems, Donna enjoys spending time with her family and making crafts. She has recently passed her motorcycle test and is looking forward to whatever adventures life brings next.

Acknowledgments

Thank you to my husband, Mark Mitchell, for setting up our garden railway, otherwise I wouldn't have these crazy stories to share.

My kids, their partners and my grandchildren for going along with my stories and giving me inspiration every day.

My mother and father who I love dearly, I am so glad my dad got to see the garden railway before he left us. He is missed every day.

To every reader who has joined in the fun, shared my stories and encouraged me to get it published.

Look out for future volumes of Confessions of Smalltown

Printed in Great Britain
by Amazon